# Most Famous Baseball Player

## Philippa Werry

illustrated by Christian Pearce

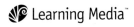 Learning Media

Jordan and I are waiting on the sidewalk for our town parade band.
The most famous baseball player in the world is riding in our town parade!
He once went to school in our town.
That's why he's riding in the parade today.

We hear the parade coming
down the street.
Jordan and I jump and shout.
We want the TV crew to film us.
Then we'll be on TV with the most
famous baseball player in the world.
Some little kids across the street
are waiting, too.
They jump and shout like we do.
"Little kids!" says Jordan.
"What would they know about baseball?"

"They might know something," I say.

The band comes down the street.
Jordan and I jump, shout,
and wave our flags.
The little kids across the street jump,
shout, and wave their flags.
"Little kids!" says Jordan.
"What would they know about baseball?"

"Well, they might know something," I say.

The clowns come down the street.
Jordan and I jump and shout.
We wave our flags and cheer.
The little kids across the street
jump and shout.
They wave their flags and cheer.
"Little kids!" says Jordan.
"What would they know about baseball?"

"Could be that they do know
something," I say.

At last, the most famous baseball player
in the world comes down the street.
He looks right at Jordan and waves to him.
He looks right at me and waves to me.
Jordan jumps and waves to him,
and so do I.
"You're the best!  You're the best!"
Jordan and I shout.
I hope the TV crew is filming us!

Suddenly the band stops.
The clowns stop.
The most famous baseball player
in the world stops.
He stops right in front of the little kids
across the street.
He gives them some signed baseballs.
He puts a little kid on each
of his shoulders.
The little kids call him Uncle.
The TV crew films them.
"Little kids!" says Jordan.
"What would they know about baseball?"

I say to Jordan,
"Those little kids might know a lot
about baseball.
The most famous baseball player in the
world is their uncle!
I'm going over to talk to them.
We just might find out something
we don't know.
If he plays baseball with them,
they might be the
best themselves one day.
And, if we're lucky, they might have
some signed baseballs to give away."